A Child's Book of
FAMILY DEVOTIONS

This Little Book Has Short Devotions for
the Family to Share

Scripture quotations in this publication are from The Holy
Bible: NEW INTERNATIONAL VERSION, copyright © 1978 by
the New York International Bible Society. Used by permission
of Zondervan Bible Publishers.

Copyright © 1983 Concordia Publishing House
3558 S. Jefferson Avenue, St. Louis, MO 63118
Manufactured in the United States of America

"...You created my inmost being;...I am...wonderfully made."

Valerie was very happy, for there was a new baby in her house. She helped her mother care for the baby. She noticed the tiny toes and the little fingers. The baby felt so small when her mother let her hold it. It was hard to believe that she was ever that small.

What is your favorite part of your body? How do your eyes work? What would happen if your feet were where your ears are?

Dear Jesus,

Thank You for making me. Thank You for my eyes to see Your beautiful world, for my ears to hear the singing of the birds. Thanks for making me special.

Amen.

"God so loved the world that...."
John 3:16

In Sunday school one morning, Mrs. Jones showed the children two pictures. One was a picture of Jesus on the cross, and another was an empty cross with an empty tomb in the background. Do you know what these pictures meant? Sure. The one with Jesus on the cross tells us how Jesus died for our sins, and the empty cross and tomb show us that Jesus rose from the dead, so that we may have life for ever and ever.

Do you believe that Jesus died for *your* sins? Do you believe that Jesus rose from the dead for *your* salvation? How much does God love *you*? How much do *you* love God?

Dear God,
Thank You for Jesus. He died for my sins and rose from the dead to give me eternal life. I am so glad that Jesus is in my heart.

Amen.

"God is love."

1 John 4:8

Do you know that God loves you? That *you* are very special to Him? Jesus even loves you when you fight with your sister or brother. He loves you when you yell at your parents or cheat in school. Jesus loves you but He is also unhappy. Why? Because He wants you to love everybody.

Why is it wrong to fight? To cheat in school? To yell at your parents? Do your parents love you even when you do wrong? Why do you need to ask Jesus and your parents for forgiveness?

Dear Jesus,

Forgive me for the wrong things I did today. I know You love me, and I will try to do better tomorrow because I love You.

Amen.

"...your sins are forgiven."

Matthew 9:2

Jimmy and Danny were playing. Danny wanted some of Jimmy's blocks, but Jimmy would not share. So Danny hit Jimmy. And Jimmy hit Danny back. Mother had to talk to both of them. She was very unhappy.

Why was the boys' mother unhappy? Were the two boys wrong? Why were they wrong? How would Jesus feel about what happened? Why?

Dear Jesus,

Forgive us when we do not share our toys. Forgive us when we hurt each other. Teach us to love each other as You love us. Help me to love my brother or sister. Help me to love You more.

Amen.

"Trust in the Lord with all your heart."
Proverbs 3:5

Susie was scared. As she lay in her bed in the darkness, she could see shadows outside her window. She could hear noises. She saw the lightning and heard the thunder. She got up and ran into the room with her mother and dad.

Her dad took her back to her room, and they looked out the window together. He showed Susie that the shadows were the trees blown by the wind. That the noise was a limb rubbing against the house. He told her that the light and noise would not hurt her. Susie was then able to sleep.

What things scare you? What can you do when you feel afraid?

Dear God,
Help me to trust in You all the time. Thank You for *always* protecting me when I am afraid. I love You.

Amen.

"...let us not love with words...but with actions."

1 John 3:18

Joe was very close to his sister. But his sister was upset. Joe was always taking her coloring books and coloring the pages before she got a chance. Or he would take her crayons without asking, and when she got them back they were broken. Joe always told Sandy that he loved her.

Was Joe really telling the truth? Is it right to take someone else's things without asking? How can we show that we really mean what we say?

Dear Jesus,
You always do what You say. Many times I do not. I am sorry. I will try to do better with Your help. I will show that I love You by the way I act.

Amen.

"Worship the Lord your God, and serve Him only."

Matthew 4:10

It is not easy to get up on Sunday morning. You play hard all day Saturday, and you are tired. Then you have to get up and get dressed and go to church. You would rather watch television and then go out and play. You get unhappy when your parents insist that you get dressed.

Why is church important? Why is Sunday school and the church service important? What things do you enjoy about going to church?

Dear God,
Forgive me when I grumble. When I go to church, I learn how much You love me. Help me to love You more and to do as my parents say. They love You too.

Amen.

"Set a guard over my mouth...keep watch over...my lips."

Psalm 141:3

Billy wondered why he did not have many friends at school. They would not let him play with them when they went out for recess. You see, Billy always said bad things about his friends. He called them names and treated them mean.

Have you ever said things that were not pleasing to Jesus? Do you say bad things to your friends? Why did Billy's classmates not want to play with him? What could Billy do to change?

Dear God,

Put good thoughts into my head. Let my mouth speak nice words to my friends. Help me to love others and to show it in what I say.

Amen.

"A friend loves at all times...."
Proverbs 17:17

Everyone watched Joey. You could count on Joey showing up when you had some candy or another special treat. Whenever there was work to be done, Joey was always too busy to help. It seemed that Joey could only be counted on when there were goodies.

Is it wrong to do something only when you get something in return? How can we show our friends that we love them? Did Jesus expect something in return every-time He did something for someone?

Dear Jesus,
Help me to show my friends that I love them. Let me help because of Your love in my heart. Teach me not to be selfish, to play fair, and to take turns. Help me to love at all times.

Amen.

"Let the word of Christ dwell in you...."
Colossians 3:16

In Sunday school one spring, all of Mrs. Summers' class planted seeds in little cups. As the weeks went by, plants appeared and then flowers. The class gave the flowers to mothers for a present. Mrs. Summers explained to the class that they should grow up to be beautiful Christians by telling others about Jesus.

How does Jesus want us to grow? Why don't you plant a seed and watch it grow? How can you show others that you are God's child?

Dear Jesus,
Help me to grow up in Your love. May I be someone beautiful for You. Thank You for the love that grows in my heart.
Amen.

"...the Lord your God loves you."
Deuteronomy 23:5

Amy liked to show people that she loved them. She made a big red heart and took it to her grandmother in a nursing home. She picked a bunch of flowers and gave them to her mother. Amy's mother asked her why she brought her the flowers. Amy said, "I want to show you how much I love you, and because Jesus wants me to show the love He has put in my heart." Amy's mother was very happy.

Do you enjoy doing things for others? What can you do to help? Do you know that God loves you? Do you love God?

Dear God,
Thank You for Your love. It makes me feel happy inside. I love You too.
Amen.

"Praise the Lord...."

Psalm 103:1

Have you ever been so happy that you wanted to shout for joy? Maybe it was because of a special present you received —or a special day when the grass was a greener green and the sky a bluer blue. Maybe it was because you knew that Jesus thinks *you* are very special. Did you want to praise the Lord for the special world God gave you?

What makes you really really happy? What do you feel when you are happy? Why should we praise the Lord?

Dear Jesus,

I want to tell the world how great You are. You are very special to me. I love You so very much.

Amen.

"Children, obey your parents in everything, for this pleases the Lord."

Colossians 3:20

Sometimes it is not easy to like things we eat. Maybe you do not like spinach or squash or some other food. Maybe you do not like to keep your room clean or to study your lessons. And you get unhappy when your parents insist that you eat, or clean, or study. They do these things because they love you. By eating good foods you get strong. By cleaning your room, you learn neatness. By studying you learn important things.

Why is it important to obey your parents? Why does this please God?

Dear God,

Thank You for giving me my parents. I am sorry when I do not obey them. I love them. I love You too.

Amen.

"If anyone loves Me, he will obey My teaching."

John 14:23

Jeff's mother had told him not to play with the kitchen knives. One day Jeff was playing with one and cut his finger. It hurt, and Jeff cried. Mother put a Band-Aid over the cut, but she was still unhappy with Jeff. God has told us to obey Him. When we disobey God we get hurt. God does not want us to be hurt. He teaches us so we will be happy and well.

Was Jeff wrong? What happened when he disobeyed? Why does God teach us?

Dear God,
Forgive me when I disobey You. I know that You want only the best for me. May I try to please You by doing as You ask.

Amen.